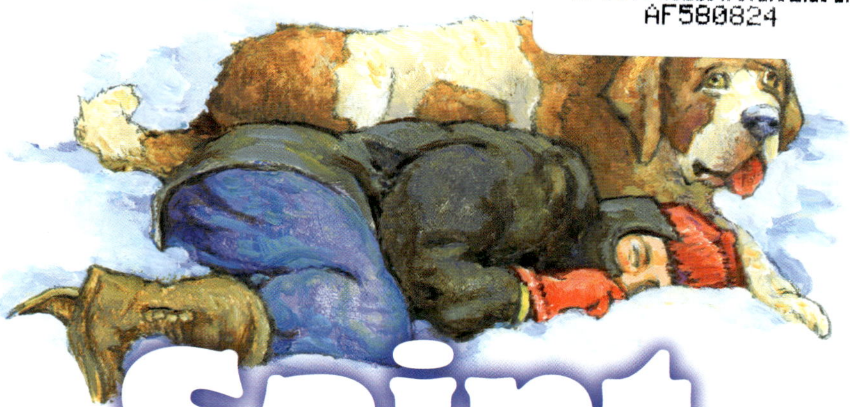

Saint Bernards

and Other Dogs That Work

by Holly Schroeder
illustrated by Troy Howell

Scott Foresman
is an imprint of

PEARSON

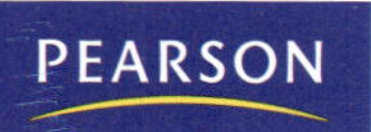

Glenview, Illinois • Boston, Massachusetts • Mesa, Arizona
Shoreview, Minnesota • Upper Saddle River, New Jersey

Illustrations
Troy Howell

Photographs
Every effort has been made to secure permission and provide appropriate credit for photographic material. The publisher deeply regrets any omission and pledges to correct errors called to its attention in subsequent editions.

Unless otherwise acknowledged, all photographs are the property of Pearson Education, Inc.

Photo locators denoted as follows: Top (T), Center (C), Bottom (B), Left (L), Right (R), Background (Bkgd).

Cover: ©Olivier Maire/Corbis; 3 (TL) ©GK Hart/Vikki Hart/Getty Images, (BL) ©Creatas/Jupiter Images, (TR, BR) Getty Images; 4 ©John Henshall /Alamy Images; 11 Courtesy, Natural History Museum of Bern, Switzerland; 15 (B) ©Juniors Bildarchiv/PhotoLibrary Group, Ltd., (CR) Courtesy, The Seeing Eye, Inc.; 16 ©Frank Siteman/PhotoEdit; 17 ©Steven King/AP Images

ISBN 13: 978-0-328-39379-4
ISBN 10: 0-328-39379-7

1 2 3 4 5 6 7 8 9 10 V010 17 16 15 14 13 12 11 10 09 08

Many dogs do brave and important work for people. Some dogs help police fight crime. Some dogs guide blind people. Other dogs cheer up people in hospitals. Dogs even **rescue** people who are lost.

Certain kinds of dogs are better at helping people than other kinds. German Shepherds, Golden Retrievers, and Labrador Retrievers are some modern dogs that help people. But the best-known stories of dogs helping people are told about Saint Bernards.

Saint Bernard

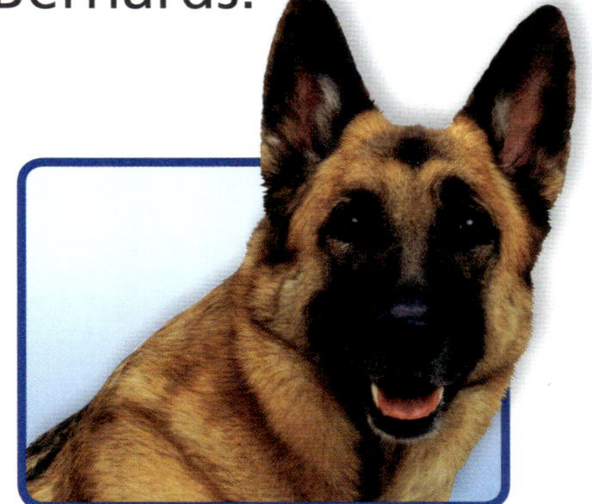

German Shepherd

Labrador Retriever

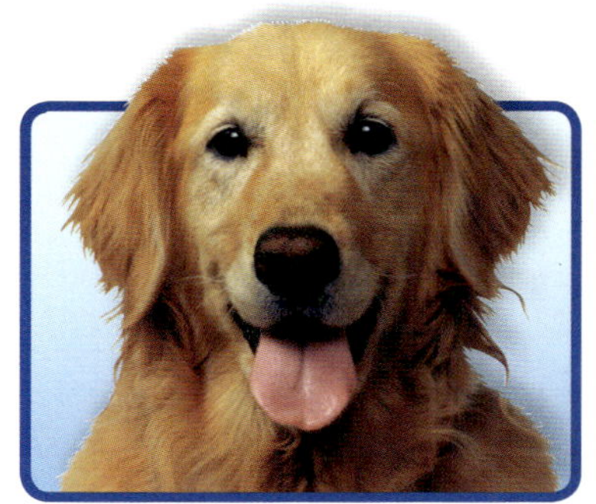

Golden Retriever

Saint Bernards

The Saint Bernard is a dog that has been doing courageous work for centuries. The story of how this special dog got its name begins in the year 1700.

At that time, the big dogs lived with **monks,** religious men, high in the Alpine Mountains of Switzerland. The monks' **monastery**—a special home—was named for Saint Bernard. The monks who lived and worked at the Saint Bernard Monastery knew that the weather in the Alps was often bad. Because the mountains were so high, there was always a lot of snow and wind.

The Saint Bernard Monastery is high in the mountains.

Anyone who wanted to travel in these dangerous mountains had to **pursue** a narrow path. This path was called The Great Saint Bernard Pass. It lies between Switzerland and Italy, and it was traveled by traders and soldiers. The bad weather made travel dangerous. Snow in the Alps can get as deep as 32 feet. Temperatures can drop to 22 degrees below zero. Falling rocks can cause avalanches when snow crashes off mountains and can bury people and even houses. All of these things made traveling very difficult.

The monks, who lived with their big guard dogs, wanted to aid travelers. They had named their big dogs Saint Bernards, after the place where they lived. Sometimes these dogs helped rescue travelers lost in the mountains. One of their Saint Bernards, named Barry, became very famous for saving people.

Like most dogs, Barry had a good sense of smell and hearing. As a Saint Bernard, though, he had other qualities. His warm fur protected him from the cold. His strong legs could dig through a lot of snow. But Barry became famous for his good **instincts**. He could sense things humans couldn't. Some people said that he even knew when a snowstorm was coming.

Barry lived with the monks from 1800 to 1814. So many stories were told about him that he became a legend. He rescued lost travelers with the monks, by himself, and with other dogs. When Barry worked with other dogs, they would search together through the snow. When they found someone, the dogs seemed to **resolve** the problem. One dog dug the person out of the snow, and another dog licked the person's face to wake him or her up. Barry would then run back to get the monks.

Popular stories told how Barry also often led people to safety through the snow. Sometimes the person that Barry found was hurt and couldn't move. Then Barry would stay with the person to keep him or her warm until the monks came. Barry's warmth helped to keep people from dying in the cold.

During his life, Barry was said to have helped save more than 40 people. Stories about him were in newspapers. For a while, he was one of the most famous dogs in the world. Once Barry was reported to have rescued a small boy who wrapped his arms around Barry's neck and held on tight. People said that Barry dragged the boy through the snow back to safety. People were very sad when Barry died in 1814.

In 1815, Barry's body was put into a museum. People can still go to see him and learn about the brave things he did. To honor him, the monks still always name one of their Saint Bernards Barry, after him.

Saint Bernards worked to save people for more than 300 years. They have saved more than 2,000 people.

The first Barry can be seen in the Natural History Museum in Berne, Switzerland.

Today, Saint Bernard dogs do not do much rescue work. Now helicopters make it easier to find lost travelers. Most Saint Bernards today are pets. They love children and are called gentle giants.

Barry was smaller and looked different than Saint Bernards alive today. Barry weighed about 100 pounds. Today's Saint Bernards weigh between 150 and 200 pounds. In fact, the largest dog that people have ever seen was a Saint Bernard. His name was Benedictine, and he weighed 305 pounds!

German Shepherds

Saint Bernards are not the only helping dogs. German Shepherds also share that honor.

Dogs have helped blind people for centuries. But German shepherds became famous in Germany for being trained to guide soldiers blinded in World War I. A wealthy American woman heard about these dogs and went to visit the school where they were trained. In 1927, she wrote about these guide dogs in a popular American magazine. A young blind man named Morris Frank heard about the dogs and decided he wanted to train one to help him "see." He lived in Tennessee, but he went to Switzerland to help train his dog. He was teamed with a female German shepherd named Buddy. Buddy became the first guide dog in the United States.

In 1929, Morris Frank founded the first school for guide dogs in the U.S. He called it "The Seeing Eye." Today more schools exist, and thousands of blind Americans use guide dogs to help them live alone. In countries all over the world, even more people use dogs to be their eyes and ears.

The Seeing Eye school still trains dogs today.

This German Shepherd can guide a blind person to safe places.

Labrador Retrievers

Golden Retrievers

The most common guide dogs today are Labrador Retrievers. These large black, yellow, or chocolate dogs are friendly, smart, and always happy to help people.

Golden Retrievers are also popular guide dogs. Like Labradors, they were trained to retrieve birds for hunters. Also like Labradors, Goldens are smart and friendly, and they love to please people.

When any guide dog is working, you should never pet it unless you ask its owner first. These dogs have been trained to pay attention to their owners and to the world around them. They are not regular pets.

Golden Retriever

Guide dogs help their owners lead better lives. It can take two years of training for a puppy to become a guide dog. These dogs must learn how to guide their owners into stores and malls. Guide dogs even ride the bus. They can't be afraid of the noise and sights of either the city or the country.

Different kinds of dogs can help people in different ways. Dogs can rescue people in the mountains or after disasters. Dogs can help people through **conflict**. Working dogs are heroes!

Labrador Retriever

Now Try This

Fact Cards About Dogs

You learned about different kinds of dogs that can help people in different ways. You can use fact cards to help you remember everything you learned. You and a partner can also use fact cards to tell how things are alike and different.

Here's How To Do It!

1. Look through this book to review the different kinds of dogs.
2. Draw a picture of a dog on a fact card. Write the name of the kind of dog you drew.
3. Write one or two facts about the dog.
4. Do the same for the other kinds of dogs.
5. Find a partner and share your fact cards.
6. Use one fact card to tell your partner about one kind of dog.
7. Have your partner use another fact card to tell you about another kind of dog.
8. Take turns telling how the dogs are alike and different.

Glossary

conflict *n.* a fight, battle, or struggle

instinct *n.* a natural way of behaving that is not learned, especially in animals

monk *n.* a man who gives his life to religion

monastery *n.* a special home for monks

pursue *v.* to follow something or someone

rescue *v.* to save someone from danger

resolve *v.* to fix or solve a problem